Legal
Protection

Legal Protection

Affordable Options for Individuals, Families, and Small Businesses

LÉONIE ROSENSTIEL

Dayspring Resources

Published by Dayspring Resources, Inc., PO Box 94057, Albuquerque, NM 87199

ISBN (paperback): 978-1-962888-00-4
ISBN (ebook): 978-1-962888-01-1

Illustrations used by permission of Shutterstock
Author Photo: C&H Productions
Book design and production by www.AuthorSuccess.com

DISCLAIMER: The material in this volume was obtained from public sources, correspondence, and private interviews. The information contained in it was accurate, to the best of my knowledge, at the time this book went into production. Nothing in this book should be construed as legal advice, as a legal opinion, or as an opinion on the outcome of any legal matter.

To all the people who would benefit from easy access to information about the law, and to on-going expert legal representation on demand that doesn't break the bank.

Contents

Foreword

Legal Protection shows you how to find expert help, as well as hope that you can successfully negotiate our byzantine legal system. Whether you need a document analyzed or are trying to understand a court process, it can help you find someone who's on your side. Even if your bank account isn't exactly overflowing with cash, the information in this book might still allow you to stop worrying about the possible future legal problems that almost all of us grapple with eventually.

Today, you want—and deserve to have—information on the companies with which you deal. Who created them? Do they have any ethical principles that they've upheld, over time? Are they simply remnants of brand names, peeking tentatively out from under the umbrella of a new controlling corporate hierarchy, their principles already changed to please their new owner? Sometimes, too, less expensive alternatives are cheaper because they're inferior. Léonie knows how to compare these offerings clearly so that you know exactly which services you're getting, and how each company compares to other companies offering services that might look superficially similar.

Over the years since I started reading Léonie's books, I've come to trust her information and her conclusions. She always does her homework, and in the pages that follow, Léonie's diligent research allows her to offer you surprising facts about the companies on the legal scene. Some of them are amusing, some are surprising.

Rarely does the writer of a preface know exactly how and why a book was written, but with this one, I do. I asked Léonie to give some hope to people whose loved ones had been scooped up into the state-run legal system. They'd become part of the institution known as "legal guardianship."

She decided to grant my request, sifting through I can't even imagine how many hundreds of sources, interviewing experts, and searching her own files, with their thousands of pages of documentation on this subject. I'm happy to say that she has finally found ways that you, and others like you, might be able to protect yourselves from the many perils of our legal system.

Earlier in my career, I was a client of LegalShield (the company profiled in Chapter I) myself. Recently, I also gave a keynote speech at their Annual Convention. As a result of that relationship and Léonie's research, I understand, first-hand, why they were rated the top firm in the field by Forbes Advisors.

Jack Canfield, Coauthor of the *Chicken Soup for the Soul*® series and *The Success Principles™: How to Get from Where You Are to Where You Want to Be*

"Third sentence, second one over ... what does that word mean?"

Do You Need Legal Help? Do You Need to File a Legal Document?

"So, sue me!" you hear someone say. Likely, that person has just made an error, expressed an unpopular opinion, or made an embarrassing comment. To defuse the situation, out comes this old semi-serious challenge, often with a shrug of the shoulders to accompany an apologetic expression. The underlying assumption is that suing is such a drastic remedy that no one would ever do it over a minor social offense.

Wrong! In the United States, just about anyone can attempt to sue anyone else. In 2019, almost 300,000 new cases found their way into the federal court system alone. By 2021, more than 755,000 cases were active (pending). The federal courts had expected an even larger caseload. They attributed lower filing numbers to the COVID-19 pandemic. According to the Institute for the Advancement of the American Legal System, more than 100 million lawsuits are filed in state courts every single year. *With just over 331 million people in the United States, it seems that more than one person out of four might well be involved in a court process during any given year!*

Not everyone who wants or needs to file a legal paper is involved in a lawsuit. Some people are buying or selling houses, setting up a small business, getting a lease, or signing a contract. However, those legal documents are often written in jargon that is hard for non-lawyers to understand. Sometimes, even if you can read the words, they either don't make sense to you or they don't mean the same thing to lawyers and the courts as they do to you.

Some states penalize residents who don't have health insurance. Most of us realize that someday, we'll need medical care in some form. Why wouldn't we also want to protect ourselves against the steep fees many lawyers charge? In many ways, it seems that having some sort of "legal insurance" ought to be like having health insurance. You know that someday, suddenly, you'll need help from a person who knows the law.

I spent ten years as a volunteer advocate for non-profit organizations. During that time, I saw many bills make their way through the New Mexico State Legislature. Most started with several pages, defining—specifically and for the purposes of that bill—terms most people would think they already understood, like "parent" or "child."

Some law firms and attorneys have joined in a recent attempt to write legal papers in ordinary English rather than "legalese." (Legalese, especially the required use of Latin and French technical terms in legal papers, has been decreasing over the past few decades anyway.) The problem with disposing of technical language is that the law thrives on precision. What one person means by "ordinary care" might not be what the next person means by that same term.

"Inertia, incompetence, status, power, cost, and risk are

a formidable set of motivations to keep legalese . . . These motivations lack any intellectually or socially acceptable rationale; they amount to assertions of naked self-interest," wrote Professor Robert W. Benson of Loyola Law School.[1]

Until all lawyers and all courts agree to create legal documents in simple English, and to clearly define what those terms are supposed to mean to all lawyers and all courts, it will continue to be difficult for a non-attorney to understand these jargon-filled legal papers.

Those at the top of the financial pyramid can afford to keep phalanxes of attorneys on retainer. "I read what you wrote, then I immediately called my attorney." That's what Jack Canfield, the multimillionaire co-author of the *Chicken Soup for the Soul®* series told me about one of my manuscripts describing how the legal system often goes wrong when dealing with adult guardianship. How many of us can do that without having to think twice about it? Do we even know an attorney we can call?

At the other end of the financial spectrum are the poor. They might be assigned a public defender (if they have been charged with a crime) or find a (free) attorney from a state-run law clinic to take their case. Indigent seniors can get help from special nonprofit law offices. I listened, recently, as the administrator of one of those "senior citizen law offices" answered an interviewer's questions. If the senior had what she referred to as "a small estate," their office would draw up a will, she said, for "only $500" if the senior's financial status was at or near the poverty line.

---

1 "Legal Quotes," https://www.plainlanguage.gov/resources/quotes/legal-quotes/, accessed October 26, 2023.

"What's a 'small estate?'" the interviewer asked.

"The highest amount of assets would be $500,000," she replied.

To attorneys, even attorneys in non-profit law offices that deal with aging seniors today, that's a *small* amount. (These law offices will not help people under sixty-five.)

Now that you know about the extremely wealthy and the poor, what about the rest of us? According to the Bureau of Labor Statistics, the average hourly wage in June 2023 was $32.18, while the average hourly legal fee for an experienced attorney was $200-$400. Most people can't afford simply to pick up the phone and spend that sort of money because they have a question about the law. This difference between what attorneys earn per hour and what the rest of us earn per hour has been causing public resentment for decades.

The counterargument to this is the venerable joke about the consultant, called in desperation when a plant stopped functioning. Its owners were losing millions of dollars per day. The consultant looked around the place, told them to change a screw, then presented them with a bill for $50,000. They followed his instructions. The plant started working again.

"What's this for?" the CEO who had escorted him around the plant countered when the consultant handed him the bill. "You were only there for fifteen minutes. All you did was tour the plant and tell us to change a screw, so I want to see a detailed bill!"

"Fine."

The consultant then presented the plant's owners with a "corrected invoice." It read, "Price of screw, $0.50. Knowing where to look and why that specific screw was the one that needed changing, $49,999.50."

What moved me to write this book? I'm not an attorney, but I am a "legal junkie." I listened as relatives talked about their legal problems. I involved myself in discussions about the law. I watched legal shows on TV. When it came my turn to be involved in a legal matter that didn't resolve for fourteen years, I ultimately had four different legal firms representing me at different times, plus several others that handled small "overflow" bits of the same case.

I've had more than a dozen "primary" lawyers take care of legal matters for me. How thrilled I'd have been to find a single firm rather than simply bouncing around from one of them to the next! Not to mention the expense of paying all those people, some of whom turned out to be a whole lot better than others. (For the record, I dedicated my book *Protecting Mama* to my last major attorney, who unfortunately has now passed away. He was one of the best.)

Most people know, instinctively, that the middle class can't afford easy access to the $1,000-plus-per-hour lawyers the elite sometimes use. On the other hand, they're not poor enough to qualify for free representation, either. Today, numerous solutions exist to help the middle class get competent legal help without going bankrupt. Harlan Stonecipher, who, after a short time as a teacher became an insurance agent, recognized this problem when he saw how much it cost him to retain an attorney after an auto accident. He set up a company to remedy the situation, and his creation, now called LegalShield, is the subject of the first chapter of this book.

In 2023, *Forbes Advisors* published a list of the five top firms offering "alternative" methods of accessing legal services that won't bankrupt you. By "alternative," I mean one or more of the following:

- Not automatically a standard hourly rate, and you might not have to see a lawyer in person

- Not a retainer

- Not automatically a per-project fee you sign up for on the website to pay for the services of an attorney who follows a project through from beginning to end

The firms *Forbes Advisor* listed are:

1. LegalShield

2. Rocket Lawyer

3. LegalZoom

4. IncFile

5. FindLaw

More than one of these companies guarantees the client a discount off their affiliated attorneys' hourly rates, and sometimes no fee at all for selected services or forms. Some of them include "upsells" to other services, like tax preparation. I'll discuss each of these five companies in its own separate chapter.

I've added three bonus chapters describing other services that combine various elements of filling out digital legal forms (often utilizing proprietary computer programs), perhaps some contact with licensed attorneys, and sometimes referrals to local attorneys, without any guarantee of discounted rates.

Some of them also include "upsells" to other services, like tax preparation. The last two—research reveals that they are the same company, after all—don't find a place on the *Forbes* list, but they have been around for a while, and readers might benefit from knowing what they offer.

This book contains no affiliate links. If you join LegalShield after a personal tour of their website, I'll get a little something. And I do mean a *little* something. You'll be treating me to the equivalent of a *Grande Caffe Americano* at Starbucks for every month you stay a member. But it will only cover that caffeine booster shot if the current Starbucks price doesn't rise, and only if I order that drink for take-out or drink it in the store.

The information that follows is neither legal advice nor an opinion about how any individual legal matter you might have will end. I'll describe each company, the products and services it provides, and how it compares to the others.

No one can predict the outcome of any legal case or promise you that any legal matter will be resolved in your favor. The fees mentioned are correct as of the time this was written but be sure to recheck the specific amounts because they might change over time. I hope that one of these options fits in with what you need now, and that this book will also provide you with the peace of mind you need, knowing that you'll have access to comparatively affordable legal help whenever you need it.

"If I tag some fan with a foul ball, does the team lawyer have my back?"

CHAPTER I

LegalShield—An Affordable Legal Insurance System

The firm now called LegalShield provides specific (and wide-ranging) legal services based on a flat monthly fee. The basic subscription often works out to cost just about as much as a monthly subscription to a local newspaper. According to HowMuchIsIt.org, a subscription to a local newspaper can run about $360 per year. The basic subscription to LegalShield costs $29.95 per month ($359.40 per year),

However, the number of subscriptions (4.6 million as of this writing) doesn't reflect the total number of people using LegalShield's services. Why? Because an entire household can use the same subscription. Suppose Susie needs a lawyer's letter written to her daughter Janie's school, but she also needs another lawyer's letter, written on her own behalf, to her employer. Then, her teenage son, Sam, gets a traffic ticket, and her husband, Tom, wants a new employment contract reviewed. The family has only one subscription, but four people are being helped. The number of people using LegalShield's services is far greater than the number of its current subscribers.

Harlan Stonecipher, as I mentioned in the Introduction, was an insurance agent when he got this idea in 1969, so it's not surprising that he structured his business to provide "legal insurance" for normal people so they can claim that service whenever they need it. Unlike the other firms described in this book, his focus was consistently on personal service from firms of attorneys who shared his philosophy. This is different from the philosophy of other services that often concentrate on helping non-attorneys fill out legal forms or providing existing attorneys who want to become affiliates with a way to market their services.

The company went through an Initial Public Offering (IPO) on the New York Stock Exchange in 1984, but was once again taken private in 2011, under the control of MidOcean, an equity firm. From what I've seen, LegalShield started out with a good business concept and continued to improve it over time. I believe that was why it won first place in the 2023 rankings. Unlike some of the other firms you'll see profiled in this volume, which have had their own legal woes, Mid-Ocean states, "The prepaid legal concept is endorsed by the National Association of Attorneys General and the American Bar Association."[2]

> **"LegalShield started out with a good business concept and continued to improve it over time."**

Below is a summary of LegalShield's basic services:

---

2 "PPLSI (LegalShield)," https://www.midoceanpartners.com/our-business/portfolio-companies/pplsi-legalshield, accessed October 26, 2023.

- LegalShield was established as a then-radical attempt to bring legal services to millions of people who, because attorneys charged so much, would otherwise avoid consulting them, even when their knowledge would be beneficial. The law firms with which LegalShield contracts are what's called "full service," meaning that multiple attorneys work there, and they handle many different sorts of legal issues.

- LegalShield only contracts directly with one firm in each state (this helps with quality-control issues, as I'll explain later). They check all new clients for conflicts of interest with existing clients. If a conflict of interest exists, they will find you another attorney licensed to practice in your state, who will agree to take an hourly fee of 25 percent less than the standard rate that the second firm normally charges.

- As of this writing, LegalShield has prospered for more than half a century. It now covers more than 4.6 million subscribers in the United States and Canada, with a range of services starting at $29.95/month. That fee would apply to all members of a family living under one roof. It reviews contracts, helps with traffic tickets, gives advice over the phone, writes letters, or makes a phone call to protect your interests. It plans estates (wills, powers of attorney, etc.) as well.

- LegalShield doesn't charge a per-hour fee for these services, or for speaking to you, unless the time spent goes over a certain limit. This limit is calculated separately for each project. As of this writing, they agree to review an unlimited number of legal documents every month. Each one can be up to fifteen pages long. After the page limit is reached, a 25 percent discount off their hourly rates kicks in.

- What does LegalShield charge extra for? Representing you in court, reviewing long documents, and complex assignments like drawing up trust documents. You get 25 percent off its normal hourly rate because you're a "member" of LegalShield. Although the contracted firm may also take other clients, LegalShield members always get priority treatment at the firm with which the company contracts to provide service in each state (and in each Canadian province).

- What are the caveats? The work covered by the monthly fee must be new, which means it's not part of a case that was in progress before you joined LegalShield. They are willing to help with an existing case, too, but again at the standard 25 percent off normal hourly rates, as described above.

- It pays you to become a subscriber before you run into a legal issue, because the LegalShield provider's current standard rate (in my area) is $300/hour. Even with the discount, that single hour of an experienced attorney's time would cost almost as much as a year's worth of premiums. They'll also help you, at the same rate, and coach you on what to say in court if you want to file forms *pro se* (without an attorney's name showing on the court records).

- Your monthly fee will never increase. When I first became aware of LegalShield's premiums (decades ago), they were $9.95 per month. In 2023, the base rate is $29.95 per month. It pays you to be loyal; those earlier subscribers are still paying $9.95.

- The law firms that have contracts with LegalShield also have attorneys who represent people accused of crimes, but all services related to criminal law go into the 25 percent discount off the hourly fee column.

- You can call a LegalShield attorney anytime, 24/7, if you are being arrested, are in an accident, or if your civil rights are in jeopardy (as might happen, for example, if someone appears at your door and says the state wants to take you into a state-mandated guardianship). As far as I can tell, LegalShield is unique in providing this service anywhere in the U.S. and Canada, not just in the state where you signed up. They promise to get back to you within eight business hours.

- I joined. For more than twenty years, the LegalShield contracted provider in New Mexico has been Davis Miles McGuire Gardner, PLLC. The firm has seventy attorneys and is known for its customer service. It holds the LegalShield contracts in New Mexico and Arizona. For my first legal project, I left a general message at the number provided. I had a non-emergency civil law question. A paralegal called back half an hour later, offering me the same confidentiality as speaking directly with an attorney. A senior partner with thirty years of experience called me about two business hours after that for more information. After reading the documents I emailed to the firm, that same attorney got back to me, exactly when he told me he would, with the advice I needed.

- We had further teleconferences and I submitted additional documents. None of this cost me anything beyond the monthly fee. In my opinion, I got great customer service. Everything was handled by phone and email. I got half an hour of the paralegal's time and about ninety minutes directly speaking with a senior partner. That's exclusive of the time he spent reading and analyzing my documents. The retail value of the time I spent speaking with the senior partner more than equaled my entire year's subscription.

- An additional feature of the basic plan is a substantial discount buying program for all LegalShield subscribers. This includes multiple categories, ranging from travel packages to clothing to psychological services. Offers vary by month, and you can create a profile that will increase the number of offers in your preferred categories.

- If you go to the website of any LegalShield associate, you'll find a list of programs offered where you live. Look in the top left-hand corner where it says "location" and change that location to your state or province. You can also find out from an associate the name of the firm—only one per state—as well as that firm's standard and discounted hourly rate. Contracted LegalShield attorney firms have decades of experience. You can research an individual partner's reputation online. Some people find the website confusing, so you're welcome to email me directly using the link at the end of this chapter; I'll arrange to have a human walk you through it and give you a website tour.

- LegalShield cancels contracts with provider law firms that get unresolved complaints or disagreements with subscribers that LegalShield believes are not satisfactorily resolved. After each time I had a consultation with the senior partner, LegalShield sent me a questionnaire asking me to evaluate the major components of the service I'd received. They do this for quality control.

- Should you need a provider in a different state, most likely you'll be able to use the legal firm with which LegalShield contracts in the second state. Again, if that firm can't handle your work for any reason, they work to find you another law firm to handle it, and again at a discount.

- The company's Better Business Bureau (BBB) score was A+ as of August 2023, and the BBB website showed thirty-four pages of complaints for various reasons. If this represents more than fifty years in business, that amount doesn't seem high to me. Other firms later in this volume are far newer and have a much higher number of published complaints. LegalShield has earned a 4.5 rating (out of five) score on Trust-Pilot.com, an internet rating service, for its work in the U.S., and 80 percent of its Canadian reviews are five-star raves.

- Legal Shield insures home-based businesses as well as "Ride Share Delivery" operations for additional small monthly supplements on top of the basic rate. Services include all paperwork and registered agents, but not tax services. Some documents are limited in number per year, with additional documents reviewed often at a $75-per-document fee; see the website for further information. Does the firm do anything else? Yes. LegalShield provides equally affordable insurance against identity theft, again for a small additional monthly fee.

My local LegalShield firm also invited me to a hybrid (online and in-person) will and trust information meeting. That online information option was a service I didn't even know they provided when I signed up for legal insurance. They draw up wills and power of attorney documents as part of the LegalShield service and will update them annually for free. (As I've said before, trust documents fall under the 25 percent discount rule.)

I interviewed LegalShield subscribers from different parts of the country and heard universally positive reviews. This was not a scientific survey, but rather a random one in which I quizzed LegalShield subscribers and associates at business meetings frequented by a wide selection of small business owners on Zoom, as well as in the breakout rooms at random Zoom business and coaching courses I took.

Certain states limit the services LegalShield is allowed to provide. Massachusetts is one of those. In five states–Alaska, New Jersey, Massachusetts, South Carolina, and Virginia– special conditions need to be fulfilled before someone signs up. Again, if you email me, I can find someone to help you.

LegalShield refers to its monthly fee as a "subscription," which means that you can easily cancel it by simply cancelling the next month's charge. Knowing that any subscription can be cancelled without penalty to the subscriber would tend to encourage staff and attorneys to provide good service, particularly since their monthly payments from LegalShield are based on the number of clients they service.

How does a LegalShield law firm make money? As with other insurance-based programs, not every subscriber will need service every month. Even when you don't need any service, the LegalShield firm still gets paid because you're a member signed up with them. So, they earn more money if they keep you out of legal trouble, or failing that, if they get your legal problems resolved as fast as they can.

Cancelling a LegalShield subscription requires written notice to the firm. This consists of an email or a snail mail letter to the Oklahoma-based company listing your subscriber number and contact information and telling them you want to cancel your subscription. If you have more than one LegalShield service to which you subscribe, you must list all the services (and the policy numbers) you are cancelling. Otherwise, they'll only cancel the one you ask them to, and will continue to bill you for the others.

Company representatives patrol the internet, looking for

any complaints people might post so they can resolve them. They invite the person who posts a complaint to contact their complaint division directly, even if that person never contacted LegalShield to register any dissatisfaction with the service earlier.

Some people object to LegalShield on the basis that it relies on multi-level marketing. This is true, in part. Current subscribers do recruit new ones. One thing people don't realize is that, with a multi-level firm as old as this one, new "associates" (as new recruits who tell others about the program are called) will not make much money.

Most who become associates today start out earning enough to buy a *Grande Caffe Americano* at Starbucks monthly for every new person they recruit for as long as that person remains a member. Prices might rise at Starbucks, but the LegalShield payment won't increase, and so it will only cover part of that *Caffe Americano*.

Low reimbursement for later recruits is standard practice for multi-level marketing companies in general. Only the early recruits automatically make great sums of money. After fifty years in business, LegalShield is no longer a "new" enterprise. Most people who recruit members now are working out of the conviction that they're helping to level the legal playing field so we all can get a fairer shake. In fact, recruiters expressly warn new associates that they're highly unlikely to get rich through their ability to sign up new subscribers.

Full disclosure: Back in the 1990s, I had a brief experience with the New Mexico branch of PrePaid Legal (what LegalShield was called prior to 2011). I cancelled my subscription after a few months because the firm they were then using could never learn to spell my name correctly. Others also complained back then, I later learned, leading LegalShield to cancel that law firm's contract and ask a different law firm to serve their New Mexico clients.

Comparing my dissatisfaction during the 1990s to my experience now shows that LegalShield pays attention to subscriber complaints and works to maintain quality control.

Some employers use LegalShield as a perk for their employees, paying the monthly subscription through payroll deductions. If subscribing through your job, you'll still have the option of continuing to use the service, should you ever leave that employer. Will the premium increase once you're out on your own? No.

In May 2020, LegalShield announced that it had saved its members almost $22 million in legal fees during 2019. "Over the last three years," the article posted on *Business Wire* stated, "LegalShield's provider law firms have recovered or received more than $75 million for plan members."[3]

Forbes Advisor describes LegalShield as offering the "best overall prepaid legal service."[4]

Since 2020, the Ohio Bar Association, the financial services and insurance company Primerica, Newit (a marketplace of 115,000 small business owners), and the business benefits provider PlanSource have all signed on with LegalShield to serve their clients, members, and employees. LegalShield is

3 "LegalShield Saved its Members over $20 Million in 2019," https://www.businesswire.com/news/home/20200529005012/en/LegalShield-Saved-its-Members-Over-20-Million-in-2019, posted May 29, 2020; accessed October 26, 2023.
4 Jessica Borgoyne, "Best Prepaid Legal Services of 2023," https://www.forbes.com/advisor/legal/best-prepaid-legal-services/, updated June 15, 2023, accessed October 26, 2023.

now reaching out to other corporations, offering their employees the firm's services, as well.

This all underlines the public's increasing need for legal services. The federal government has enacted more than 30,000 statutes. They add up to more than 180,000 pages, with more added almost daily. New York State's laws alone run to some ninety volumes. Is there any wonder that so many people find themselves involved in lawsuits? Eventually, just about everyone will either be involved in a lawsuit, need an attorney's advice to draw up a legal document, or want a lawyer's help to understand a legal document.

For more information about LegalShield, email me at: l.rosenstiel1@gmail.com

"My startup could really use
a pioneer type like you!"

CHAPTER II

Rocket Lawyer—The Business Form Provider with a Few Special Perks

Rocket Lawyer's founder originally carved out for himself the mission of making legal services accessible to start-up businesses. Established in 2008, Rocket Lawyer is a "new kid on the block" compared to LegalShield. It will provide you with hundreds (more like thousands) of free legal forms that you can fill out at your leisure, provided that you sign up for its underlying subscription service after a short subscription trial.

Charley Moore, who founded the company, was a Silicon Valley lawyer who began his career by representing business start-ups. He says that more than 30 million people have started Rocket Lawyer accounts over the years. Two of the "business start-ups" he advised when he was practicing as an attorney (at least they were small, at the beginning) were Yahoo! and WebTV. The firm soon made it into the *Inc* 500 list of the fastest-growing private companies.

If you are seriously unhappy about what happens after you fill out one of Rocket Lawyer's forms, you can apply for a refund, but resolution is on an individual and single-issue basis. Like traditional attorneys, they do not guarantee that your legal problem will be resolved in your favor. As of this writing, you can cancel your subscription with either a call or an email.

What they do provide:

- An attorney to speak with you for an initial interview of thirty minutes before you fill out each form. The firm says it will build a custom document based on that information. Since the laws vary from state to state, this is important.

- They will also provide some advice about filling out any of the numerous forms you can download off their website. How extensive is the "help?" I'm guessing (since I haven't used this service) that they are careful to observe the line between helping you fill out a form and giving legal advice.

- You may sign the forms (and have others sign the forms) electronically. That used to be a special service, but during Covid, this practice has become more and more common. Many court papers, deeds, and other legal papers are now routinely filed electronically.

- If needed, Rocket Lawyer will provide an attorney to "defend" the validity of the form you signed. Might they have had experience with people denying their forms' validity? At least they are willing to step up and help should that happen to you. As with all insurance and legal contracts, it's always wise to see exactly what's covered and what the specific exclusions are.

- They maintain a "network" of attorneys, but do not tell you who they are. Unless you sign up, you will not find

> "If needed, Rocket Lawyer will provide an attorney to 'defend' the validity of the form you signed."

out whether they are solo practitioners or small law firms, or perhaps larger firms. Since Rocket Lawyer claims that lawyers in their network offer a 40 percent discount off the attorneys' normal fees, in my opinion, it's unlikely that a large law firm or a well-established lawyer could afford to offer that big a discount. Either that or there's a significant mark-up before the price cut.

- There's a "discounted" annual rate of $239.99 for the first year to gain access to their forms, and $39.99 per month thereafter. That would amount to just under $480 for a basic subscription, and it would cover only your business matters. The firm now does a robust (and recurring) business providing tax services to clients who sign up for the annual subscription, but it costs extra (amount not listed on the website).

- Rocket Lawyer will provide a trademark or patent attorney. These practitioners claim to offer "half off" to members (but remember that you are already paying for your annual subscription when you contract for their work).

- If you're a new member, they will file an LLC (limited liability company) application for you for free. After that, you get "25 percent off." Since the cost is not specified, it's hard to know what the initial fee would have been or what you will be paying. In some states, it is not expensive to file, and this offer (to me) doesn't mean you're getting all that much.

- Registered agent services are also provided, at a 25 percent discount off normal rates. Delaware is a popular venue where out-of-staters start corporations and must then maintain a presence through a "registered agent." As of this writing, it costs about $100 per year to have an LLC there. So, you'd be paying about $75 instead of $100. (I got these figures from an attorney who was not associated with Rocket Lawyer or any of the other firms profiled in this volume. He was simply quoting me the usual fee in Delaware for this service.)

- They will now supply a group legal insurance policy for employees of corporations (if you leave that job, you will almost certainly lose these benefits). In 2022, they began a partnership with the New York Stock Exchange-listed Select Quote to extend services to consumers, as well. It might take time to assess the success of this project.

- Charges for specific services and document filings vary. These are in addition to the monthly fee for access to the forms. Some forms (for instance, the form to apply for a business tax identification number) are free if you ask an IRS office, and may be filed directly with the IRS, also for free. Anyone starting a business can do this, but Rocket Lawyer will charge extra to file this form for you.

- It looks as if many people forget that when they sign up

for a "trial subscription," if not quickly cancelled it will automatically convert into a paid annual subscription. (The last "trial period" I saw offered lasted only seven days!) I found multiple complaints on the internet from subscribers insisting that they thought they were only authorizing a one-time charge because they wanted to obtain a specific form.

- The attorneys with whom Rocket Lawyer works are not on staff. They are considered part of a "network" of providers to whom Rocket Lawyer refers their customers. These lawyers are "affiliates," and the specific terms of their affiliate agreements are not public. You would be personally hiring a lawyer/law firm if you use one of the affiliates in their network.

- Charges fall into several different categories. They can pyramid, and sometimes end up far greater than the subscription charges.

- Rocket Lawyer has an A+ rating from the Better Business Bureau. They do answer people who register complaints there; I found thirteen web pages of answered complaints on that site when I searched. The gist of most of the answers I saw was, "No, we don't provide that service," or "No, you misunderstood." As for Trustpilot.com, it shows an overall rating of 4.5. The reviews break down this way: about 50 percent from the U.S., followed closely by the U.K. (about 30 percent), about 10 percent from Australia, and the rest from various other countries (including ten from Qatar).

In July 2017, a committee of the New Jersey Supreme Court outlawed Rocket Lawyer, declaring that any New Jersey lawyer who became affiliated with it was doing something unethical. Not until 2021 did the New Jersey State Supreme Court rule that attorneys who were *not* licensed in New Jersey had the right to give legal advice out of their New Jersey homes to people referred by Rocket Lawyer. They were simply denied the right to say that they were licensed to practice law in New Jersey. Are there groups of Rocket Lawyer affiliates living in New Jersey who are licensed only in other states? Am I the only person who finds this ruling confusing and potentially problematic?

The New Jersey issue seemed to revolve around Rocket Lawyer not having registered with the Administrative Office of the Courts, as required by New Jersey law, as a "legal services plan." Rocket Lawyer did not tell the State of New Jersey what it paid to the attorneys who participated in its open Q & A service for subscribers, but that did not seem to be a major issue.

During the Covid pandemic, Rocket Lawyer partnered with the State of Utah. They developed what the company referred to as a two-year pilot program, a beta version of coverage to provide legal insurance to residents. That was when Rocket Lawyer reached out, for the first time, to the consumer market. For them, it was an experiment and an excursion into unfamiliar waters. But they were waters that LegalShield had been navigating for decades, and Rocket Lawyer was partnering with a state rather than relying on individual associates.

Website: https://www.rocketlawyer.com/

CHAPTER III

LegalZoom—Forms with a Tax and Lawyer Matching Service

Taiwan-born Brian Liu, founder of LegalZoom, like Stonecipher and Moore, shattered the long-held belief that you had to visit an attorney's office and pay a lot of money to get any legal work accomplished. Like Moore, Liu started out as an attorney himself. He ended up with a $2 billion NASDAQ-listed company (Symbol: LZ) that had 1,000 employees.

Established in 2001, LegalZoom created ten discrete divisions from the beginning. These ranged from intellectual property to estate planning and business creation. For nine years, it remained an online technology company, creating a network of referral attorneys only in 2010. By 2020, it had added a tax division, too. Even though the firm now has offices in California and Texas, you will never need to visit the office of the attorney or accountant providing your advice.

The companies profiled in this book state that they started for similar reasons—to make legal help accessible to most people who would normally not be able to afford to employ attorneys on staff or on retainer.

Here is what LegalZoom does, and how it is different from LegalShield:

- You pay LegalZoom for each service it provides. Each form is charged separately. It also offers "Economy," "Standard," and "Express Gold" business packages. These vary depending on the level of service LegalZoom provides and its speed. No state filing fees are included in any of the business packages. You pay extra for them. The more economical the package chosen, the longer the time you should expect it to take. As of this writing, "Economy" service is $149, "Standard" costs $329, and "Express Gold" is $349.

- Because of the per-service policy, there is no "base fee" or "subscription" service charge, only the charge for the specific legal document LegalZoom provides.

- What they call "estate plan bundles" start at $249. You will not see an attorney from the beginning to the end of this process. The same is true for starting a trust, which costs $399. A financial power of attorney and a living will (which is also called an "advance healthcare directive") are included at no extra cost. Each plan now comes with an annually renewable way to get any questions about your will answered. Cost: $199 per year.

- LegalZoom specifically states that the forms of wills and trusts will follow the requirements of your state. Just remember that these can change, so if you signed a will ten years ago, and your "subscription" lapsed, your will might no longer conform to the best practices in your state.

- In 2015, I tried LegalZoom. I filled out a will on their website and had it notarized. Then I showed it to an attorney I trusted. He said, "I'm surprised! This is a valid legal document." Back then, I saw no offer by that firm to answer questions, nor did I later subscribe to the question-answering service, and so I wonder whether that will would still be equally valid today.

- If you want to pay less, you can unbundle will and trust offers and create single documents instead (for example, powers of attorney or living wills).

- Here's why I wonder whether documents will always be valid: In 2020, I asked a different attorney to sample LegalZoom's website to see whether the legal forms posted there were current and would hold up under a legal challenge. He told me that, while many were, some weren't, and he would suggest that people be cautious about assuming that all of them would be accepted. I couldn't pay him to examine the thousands of documents on the website, just a comparatively few selected ones from his home state. I have no way of knowing whether all documents are now up to date or not.

- You will fill in forms online to customize your documents. If you are adept at answering online questions, you should manage to get something like what you thought you wanted.

- LegalZoom also offers a subscription plan (billed semi-annually or annually). It costs less than LegalShield but also offers less. For instance, where LegalShield agrees to review a fifteen-page legal document for free as part of a $29.95 monthly subscription, LegalZoom offers to review a ten-page legal document for free as part of a $19.84 monthly subscription. LegalZoom charges in advance, either $199 for a six-month period ($19.84/month) or $119 for a year ($16.54/month), whereas LegalShield billing is uncomplicated and monthly only. (These amounts were correct when last viewed.)

- Attorneys who are LegalZoom affiliates agree to work for 25 percent off their standard fees. They're not employed by LegalZoom directly. The attorney may be "affiliated" with LegalZoom in two ways. One is to serve, at stated times, for simple consultations with plan members in their state. The other is to list themselves in the directory of affiliated attorneys provided to members. Attorneys consulting online will refer complex questions to attorneys listed in the directory.

- Again, larger firms and attorneys with thirty years of experience probably won't sign up to provide these services. They are considered practice-building activities. LegalZoom states that it only allows attorneys with legal experience to become affiliates. But how much experience? One California attorney whose photo I saw on the website (last name not given) is said to have eight years of legal experience. You will likely be referred to a solo practitioner or small group law office, or perhaps to a very junior member of a larger firm.

- LegalZoom states that it has helped over 4 million people, primarily individuals and small businesses.

- LegalZoom has an A+ rating from the Better Business Bureau. There are 110 pages of complaints for this twenty-four-year-old firm on the Better Business Bureau's website. Trustpilot.com separates its U.S. and U.K. reviews, giving the U.S. operation a 4.6 but the U.K. branch only a 3.2. It received 1,134 complaints during the past three years. Of those, it closed (resolved) 363 during the past twelve months.

> "LegalZoom states that it has helped over 4 million people, primarily individuals and small businesses."

The North Carolina Bar Association (NCBA) sued LegalZoom in 2008, claiming it was providing legal advice and practicing law without a license. Eventually, eight state bar associations sued LegalZoom, but LegalZoom and its brother online legal form firms started winning, and winning big, in 2014. The firm agreed to show all its document templates to lawyers licensed in North Carolina. (No clarity on whether it needed to keep up with changes in North Carolina laws and rules and to resubmit a new template each time anything was changed.) Another requirement: They had to state these forms did not substitute for using a real, live attorney.

Prior to the settlement, LegalZoom had sued the NCBA in federal court. They claimed $10.5 million in damages on an anti-trust complaint. They said the Bar was trying to unfairly stop anyone but their own licensed attorneys from providing information in the state.

Similar complaints existed in other states, ranging from California to Arkansas to Missouri. LegalZoom prevailed.

I have no complaints about my own experience with LegalZoom. However, as I've said, according to the second attorney I consulted to vet their forms, there is a question about whether the forms posted are current. I have also read a few internet complaints written by unhappy clients who thought they were going to receive many more services than turned out to be included. Another issue they mentioned was that phone-in question time seemed to be strictly rationed.

I'm guessing that people tend to forget the "we give you one-half hour of time per month for questions" caveat I saw on the website. Unlike the policies I saw with LegalShield, I found no company representatives browsing the internet and searching for unhappy clients whose problems they then tried to resolve. They seem to have quite a few unanswered complaints.

Website: https://www.legalzoom.com/

CHAPTER IV

Incfile—The Business "Information Provider" with a Tax Referral Service

Created by hip-hop musician Dustin Ray and former firefighter Nick Siha, Incfile is another company dedicated to helping business startups. Most firms trying to offer reasonable legal fees target businesses rather than individuals. Perhaps more entrepreneurs-in-waiting than members of the public realize from the beginning that they will be required to file legal papers and need legal backup.

By 2022, Incfile was proud to report that it had created more than 1 million LLCs since it opened in 2004. Its founders, separately, had discovered how difficult (and expensive) it could be to set up an LLC when they tried to become entrepreneurs. They make clear on the website that they have no interest in providing legal representation to anyone. Their disclaimer states: "Visitors or recipients of this information should not act upon this information without consulting with legal counsel."[5]

---

5 "Incfile Legal Disclaimer and Terms of Service," https://www.incfile.com/disclaimer , accessed October 26, 2023.

This makes me wonder how they got onto the *Forbes Advisor* list of reasonable legal services, because they state, in writing, that they do not offer any legal services.

The firm expressly disclaims any responsibility for the accuracy or completeness of information/forms found on their website. By using the site, you are also granting Incfile the right to use, for its own purposes, whatever you might post.

Incfile's owners express pride in having bootstrapped their way to success, as did some of the other services profiled in this book. The co-founders say they are providing a service to others that they wish had been available when they were starting their firm. They handle business matters only:

- Documents that create new companies. For a full list, consult the website linked at the end of this chapter. Entities mentioned include LLCs, S corporations, C corporations, and nonprofit corporations.

- Documents that manage companies and change their by-laws/operating agreements. These include corporate reports, any applications for the right to do business in other states, and so on.

- Documents that dissolve corporations or reinstate corporations.

"The firm expressly disclaims any responsibility for the accuracy or completeness of information/forms found on their website. By using the site, you are also granting Incfile the right to use, for its own purposes, whatever you might post."

- The company sells a package that pays for business license research for a hopeful entrepreneur. There is a separate "research" charge. From the internet comments I have seen, this involves a delay in processing the rest of the paperwork. (Or is it now all "digital work?")

- Trademark research and trademarking are other offered services.

- Incfile charges for some services that business owners might get free elsewhere (like a business tax number–EIN), a process already familiar from prior services profiled in this book.

- As of this writing, Incfile states on their website that they offer a free tax consultation. It seems as if this might lead new businesses to sign up for the ongoing services Incfile offers.

- The first year of "registered agent" representation is supposed to be included in several of the firm's packages. (For more information, see below.)

- Research material linked on the website compares the various types of corporate structures, LLC, and incorporation information, listed by state. Bonus (free) offerings will inform you about sales tax, help you calculate your own business tax (if you want to), and more.

- There is no single, transparent listing of fees. Some vary with state fees, which are in addition to the fees charged for filing the forms themselves. They are piggybacked. You must input your specific requirements to obtain a quote.

- Incfile services will match you with an accountant, then charge a monthly fee for business accounting, tax preparation, and tax filing. If the accountant splits any of the money with Incfile, accounting ethics require this to be divulged to the client. It might be that the fee a client pays to Incfile to have access to the accountant is entirely separate from whatever fees that professional charges the client. That might avoid any ethical problems for the accountant, but I couldn't find this out on their website.

- Start-up entrepreneurs might be interested in Incfile's extensive blog. As of this writing, that ninety-four webpage puppy includes more than 900 subjects ranging from how multitasking diminishes your effectiveness at work, to the status of legislation allowing federal small business loans, to the ideal legal structure for your business.

- Incfile maintains a social media presence on YouTube, Twitter (now X), Facebook, and Instagram.

- The company wants clients to share their success stories for inclusion on the corporate website under the heading "INCspiration Stories." The photos accompanying these profiles suggest that the firm's clients are almost exclusively under the age of forty. This is the ultimate in creating a community of young entrepreneurs, which is how the company itself describes this webpage. It's a form of in-house social media.

- Note that if you choose a package to make sure your business remains in compliance with your state requirements, registered agent charges will be automatically renewed. As of this writing, that will cost at least $119 per year.

- The ten pages of complaints on the Better Business Bureau website show numerous unresolved complaints. Incfile is not accredited by the Better Business Bureau. However, Incfile has a Trustpilot score of 4.7. Go figure!

Some people have mentioned in internet reviews that they found the website hard to use. I wonder whether they are older people because the website itself feels trendy and young. In addition, their material is likely all posted, but in specialized areas. If you don't know where to look or what they're calling the subject, you're apt to find it hard to use.

Incorporating, acquiring business licenses, filing for a tax number, and so on, if charged for separately, might easily pyramid. Scrolling back through recent complaints posted on the internet, this seems to be the most frequent problem clients experienced, followed by the difficulty of finding a human to discuss things with. There are some complaints, but none of them have been answered by the company. I also saw a couple of people reporting up-charges, and even one client who said he'd been charged for the first year when Incfile was serving as his registered agent, even though the website had promised otherwise. Since the company made no comment on any of these, it's hard to know whether they might someday resolve these problems.

As *Forbes Advisor* notes, most of the information on this website is available for free if you're willing to take the time to find it. I've seen a few people complaining on the internet that their total charges ultimately amounted to $300 or $400; far more than they'd expected.

Incfile forwards state and federal government fees within twenty-four hours. The client must get any cancellations to the company (on the website) in time. Please note that they do not refund any fees you give them to send to government entities after they send those fees to that entity. They do not refund trademark fees. Cancellation fees also apply, assessed on top of orders that have been dropped. Hundreds of words modify and permit Incfile to make all decisions relative to refunds or chargebacks. Please read them carefully, because the company states that it reserves the right to change them at any time, with or without notice to its clients.

All subscriptions renew automatically. Be sure to consult all terms and conditions so you know what you are agreeing to, and to recheck the terms periodically. I'm saying this because many of the instructions I read are not being followed by people complaining about Incfile's services on the internet. It's possible that they misunderstood Incfile's terms. Either that, or Incfile changed its terms of service after a particular client signed up and that client didn't recheck before placing an order. I'm deliberately giving Incfile the benefit of the doubt here.

This is the basic problem: The terms are so extensive that you might need to hire a lawyer to interpret them for you, which was exactly what most people turned to Incfile's services to avoid.

Finally, Incfile has suit-proofed itself by including an arbitration clause in its terms of service. This prevents a client from taking the firm to court and making any dispute public. This will allow the firm to always tell the truth if it claims that no client has ever sued it. I doubt that it will ever want to change that section, so you need to know this before you start.

Website: https://www.incfile.com/

"Does anyone know this month's Click Thru Rate?"

CHAPTER V

Findlaw—Do It Yourself or Find a Lawyer

Next-to-last on the *Forbes Advisor* list comes Findlaw, a Silicon Valley firm created in 1995 by Stacy Stern, Martin Roscheisen, and Tim Stanley. Back then, they decided to create a directory of law librarians and then posted it on the internet. The three partners were reviving an earlier service called LawFinder, says the website wisemedia.ca.

Stern, a legal rebel, always wanted to make what she calls "basic law" accessible to everyone. Her second co-founder was Roscheisen, an Austrian-American tech wiz. The third co-founder, Stanley, is also an attorney with a legal philosophy like Stern's. (The basic problem, as I explained in the Introduction, is this: Even when a person can read a legal document, most members of the public have trouble understanding the meaning of many documents written in legalese, as court filings and judges' decisions tend to be.)

Stern and Stanley now work for a firm that helps lawyers gain more clients. It also posts legal papers online to make legal research easier.

In 2001, Westlaw, a self-described "legal research platform" owned by Canadian conglomerate Thompson-Reuters, long a provider of services for the legal profession, bought out Findlaw. It kept the brand name. The current Findlaw specializes in two areas—business law and estate planning. This site contains enormous quantities of free information, making more than 37,000 research topics available to the user. Would you know where to look or what you needed to know? If you don't already know exactly what you need, you might get lost in the virtual stacks of data.

> "The current Findlaw specializes in two areas—business law and estate planning. This site contains enormous quantities of free information, making more than 37,000 research topics available to the user."

The home page makes clear that FindLaw services two groups, kept a bit separate. One consists of legal professionals seeking a way to research cases. They are immediately diverted to the web page link marked "For Legal Professionals."

The rest of us would look for subjects listed on the original home page, with links leading to the following categories of material:

- Find a Lawyer

- Legal Forms and Services

- Learn About the Law

- Laws and Court Decisions

- Blog

Since the first tab encourages members of the public to "find a lawyer," this is not a consumer DIY site in the usual sense. It's primarily one that gives certain lawyers and firms featured listings. If you use FindLaw's lawyer search function, you are urged to consider location, cost, and years in business for those in the directory. These are normal considerations.

I sampled a few of the listings. No costs (per hour or per project) are given. Many firms I would have expected to see in certain categories don't show up in the directory at all. In more than one instance, a "divorce" attorney is listed as an "elder law" attorney, and the user would have to read far into the firm's profile to learn about this confusion.

As is usual for a lawyer-matching service that costs the consumer nothing, someone else must pay the bill to maintain this complex website and all the personnel to handle a set of huge databases. After doing some research, I discovered that the money to run the website and match attorneys and clients is coming out of the lawyers' pockets. FindLaw will provide attorney websites (as of this writing, at a cost of $250-$5,000 per month).

If an attorney will be paying FindLaw $60,000 per year for a website, what's the likelihood that you, should you choose to become a client, are going to get any meaningful discount off that attorney's hourly fee?

FindLaw charges attorneys for other services, too. The following information is posted on a site run by the digital agency Majux.[6] The free law resources are all great, Majux tells readers. However, many of them are links to databases run by other providers, so they are also available elsewhere. Furthermore, attorneys who cancel FindLaw's website management may find that their entire website vanishes. They cannot transfer it to any other place on the internet, because Findlaw owns it. FindLaw, Majux reports, has contracts that are awfully difficult for lawyers to get out of.[7] (Oh, the irony!)

Majux writes that FindLaw's "pay-per-click" service for attorneys works out to cost the attorney $900 per click. Not per client. Nominally, FindLaw says it only charges $150, but Majux completed a study of how many of these result in clients hiring the firm they contacted, and factored that in, too. A profile listing in the directory costs $158 per month (there may be as many as nineteen of these before the general listings in various popular legal categories).

When you start adding up $5,000 per month for a website, $158 per month for a profile listing, and $900 per click for ad links, you are talking about some very serious money. If the lawyer doing the advertising wants to stay in business, these costs must be passed on to that law firm's clients somehow. So, while FindLaw offers generous free research opportunities to lawyers and to the public, the attorneys whose featured profile listings and websites you find there probably can't afford to offer *you, the consumer,* lower fees.

In 2022, the American Bar Association claimed there were

6 "Should Your Firm Use Findlaw? Is It Legit?" https://www.majux.com/should-your-law-firm-use-findlaw/ , posted October 28, 2022, accessed October 26, 2023.
7 "Findlaw Took My Website Down. What Can I Do?" https://www.majux.com/did-findlaw-take-your-website-down/ , posted May 18, 2020, accessed October 26, 2023.

1.3 million attorneys practicing in the United States.[8] According to Lawrank.com, FindLaw claims to list more than 1 million.[9] Feel free to do your own math to figure out how much money FindLaw earns annually from its listed attorneys. That's going to be difficult, because Findlaw does not seem to post a full list of its services to lawyers and what each of them costs.

I checked some New Mexico listings. Many of the firms that I know have been in business here for decades don't figure in the directory. Maybe they just don't want to pay the listing and ad fees. The firms in the listings I checked had very few client reviews (generally fewer than five). The directory includes star ratings.

One thing that might concern you is that FindLaw warns that data input on its website or shared with attorneys in its directory might not be "secure." If so, confidentiality might be something you can't expect to get on this site. The advertising agreements cause the listings for firms with profile boosts to appear in multiple cities and counties, even when they only have offices in one city. This might confuse potential clients.

FindLaw might also contract with a law firm to produce content for the law practice's website—blogs, white papers, and the like. It's not the law firm writing these documents, it's FindLaw. If the law firm is honorable, it will review this content prior to posting to make sure it expresses the firm's beliefs and philosophy.

8 "ABA National Lawyer Population Survey: Lawyer Population by State 2022," page 1, https://www.americanbar.org/content/dam/aba/administrative/market_research/2022-national-lawyer-population-survey.pdf, accessed October 26, 2023.
9 "Your FindLaw Profile: Why It Matters and How to Get It," https://lawrank.com/your-findlaw-profile-why-it-matters-and-how-to-get-it/, accessed October 26, 2023.

One law practice I found listed under "elder law" is a personal injury firm that also handles nursing home abuse. That's a rather specialized area of practice, and not a general "elder law" attorney firm at all.

According to the subject listings, FindLaw provides attorneys in every possible legal category.

Under the DIY category, FindLaw sells legal forms and packages. An estate planning package (including a will, a HIPAA release form, and powers of attorney) currently starts at $135. You can get a plain old will form for $79. FindLaw will not complete, or help you complete, the documents it generates. Instructions for making the will legal (witnesses, notary, etc.) are included, and you need to follow them to make the will and any other documents you buy from them legally enforceable. My computer claims that the linked business forms web page contains malware and won't let me access it.

The tab "Cases and Court Decisions" only takes you to the "most popular" state courts, which means that only California, Florida, New York, and Texas are covered. FindLaw separates its blogs into subject categories. Most likely, anyone with the time to read all the educational material on FindLaw's website is not doing any other productive work.

Members of the public may also take out paid subscriptions. From the material I've read, it's unclear to me what the fees are and which additional research materials they cover.

What about reviews? As for the BBB site, the FindLaw page states, in big, red letters, that this firm is "not accredited." It goes on to tell readers that, based on the customer ratings it has, the firm has been given a 1.07 rating (out of five) by those clients who posted reviews. Altogether, Findlaw has "closed" sixty-eight complaints within the past three years, twenty-one of those within the past twelve months. All the Trustpilot.com reviews are listed as "invited," which suggests that Findlaw went out and specially requested these individuals to leave a review. (Other reviews I found on Trustpilot did not contain the notation that those other firms had invited anyone to post a review, which suggested to me that all the reviews for the other firms were spontaneous.)

Website: https://www.findlaw.com/

"Ooo, two strays to add to the database."

CHAPTER VI

Avvo—A Directory, Pro Bono Service, and Advertising Opportunity for Lawyers

Founded in the state of Washington in June 2007, just like FindLaw, Avvo also originally had three partners—Mark Britton, Paul Bloom, and Sendi Widjaja. The firm's name is derived from the Italian word for "lawyer" (*avvocato/avvo-catessa*). Avvo's founders and their advisors were associated with such internet powerhouses as Expedia and Zillow. The story goes that Britton himself was on vacation in Italy when he conceived the idea of creating an internet marketplace for lawyers, which was Avvo's primary mission.

Like Findlaw, Avvo's site also contains an extensive library of answers to general legal questions. The lawyers who participate in this part of the website are all working *pro bono*. It's part of their desire to give back to the community, we're told. However, they will not offer any legal advice on your specific case, and so are merely "educating" the public and not "advising" anyone on legal matters. You can post new questions, but you can't use personal details from your case (if you have one).

The American Bar Association's survey of attorneys claimed that on January 1, 2022, there were 1,317,010 attorneys in the United States. This included all states and territories. Its 2021 survey had listed 1,317,900. (I've seen this statistic quoted slightly differently, depending on the source, but the numbers I see are always very close to these numbers.)

Avvo gives all attorneys an Avvo profile whether they want one or not. It claims to be the largest database of attorneys, with 1.5 million listees. If this is true, then Avvo lists almost 200,000 attorneys more than the number of licensed lawyers in the country. Because of the way Avvo's listings are culled from other public sites, I can guess that the same person might appear more than once, particularly if that lawyer moved into a new office recently or might be licensed in more than one state, maintaining an office or mail drop in each one.

> "Avvo gives all attorneys an Avvo profile whether they want one or not. It claims to be the largest database of attorneys, with 1.5 million listees. If this is true, then Avvo lists almost 200,000 attorneys more than the number of licensed lawyers in the country."

There is no guarantee that contact information is accurate or recent unless the listees have "claimed" their listings. I looked for an attorney I used to know. His unclaimed listing is still on Avvo. He died in 2020. The directory will demote an attorney from a paid to an unpaid listing, but I wonder what it takes to get an attorney's name removed from Avvo's list.

According to Chris Dreyer, CEO and founder of Rankings. io, there is no way to get a lawyer profile deleted from Avvo. How many listees are either retired or have passed away? Only lawyers with claimed listings may be ranked by verified clients on a scale of one to ten.

"Superb" rankings, Avvo says, are in the 9.1-10 range, and 8.1-9 is "excellent." This means that 7.1-8 would be an "okay" ranking. When I attended school, eight out of ten often was a B, which translated into "above average," not "excellent." If you got six out of ten, you were not "average"—it meant that you almost didn't pass the course at all. In other words, 6.1-7 should mean "below average." A 7.1-8 would mean "average." However, Avvo considers anything above *five* to be good. This might simply be another bit of evidence that lawyers often redefine ordinary words to mean something different from what most people mean when they use them in everyday speech.

The directory part of Avvo's site cautions against becoming the client of attorneys with a ranking under five. The lack of a ranking on unpaid listings means Avvo found the attorney or law firm mentioned somewhere on the internet, and these professionals do not choose to pay for their listings. This lack of stars and reviews might have no bearing on their ability to help any specific client. The attorney or firm might be extremely accomplished.[10]

Several attorneys from a single firm might be ranked, or only one might be. You never know.

---

10 William Pfeifer, "The 5 Biggest Reasons Why Lawyers Hate Avvo Reviews," https://www.liveabout.com/avvo-criticism-lawyers-2151218, posted February 5, 2019, accessed October 26, 2023, and "Is the Avvo Lawyer Service Legit?" https://clearwaylaw.com/avvo-lawyer-service-legit, accessed October 26, 2023. (Clearway is an Avvo competitor.)

Avvo cautions readers (in highly visible red type) against every attorney who has ever received a letter of non-compliance of any sort from any state bar, whether they asked/paid to be Avvo listees or not. All are disciplinary matters, but not all disciplinary matters are created equal. This editorial policy has led many attorneys to protest. Not filing proof of continuing education on time might result in a letter of non-compliance from the state bar. So might stealing from clients. Are both infractions equally serious? This does seem a bit like firing off a cannonball to kill a mosquito.

Justicia, another "lawyer matching" site not on the *Forbes* list, currently posts a complaint against Avvo on its website. Two Seattle attorneys sued Avvo in U.S. District Court back in 2007, claiming, "thousands of lawyers have suffered damage to their professional reputations by Avvo's publication of capricious and arbitrary ratings to consumers via the internet."

What Justicia doesn't tell you is that they ultimately lost based on Avvo's free speech rights, but this was not the end of the story. Many attorneys continue to object to Avvo's policies.

Another attorney, claiming that Avvo had permanently damaged his reputation by refusing to delete the big red caution long after he came into compliance with the requirements of his state law board, started a protest website. And the list goes on.

As complaints were increasing, Avvo managed to raise over $10 million from venture capital firms.

Repeated class-action suits and other attempts to induce Avvo to change its rating system, particularly what the lawyers involved saw as suggestions that certain attorneys were either subpar or perhaps unethical, all seem to have failed.[11] The Washington decision is often cited. Other cases Avvo won also remind everyone of Avvo's right to have an opinion, based on its own private criteria, and to express its own conclusions in public.

Not the court, but the New Jersey Bar Association joined several other state bars in 2017 when it told member attorneys that participation in Avvo violated state ethical standards, instructing its members not to participate. The bar complained that Avvo took a percentage of the money paid by clients brought to a firm by Avvo, and this amounted to "fee sharing," which is unethical in the legal profession. Similar sorts of arrangements had previously been found unethical in Ohio, Pennsylvania, and South Carolina according to the American Bar Association's *Journal*.

Avvo continued to raise money—more than $132 million through 2017, suggesting that it wanted to "go public" on the stock exchange. In January 2018, the original investors were instead bought out by a company called Internet Brands, the same firm that also created WebMD. The purchase price was not disclosed.

GeekWire, which keeps track of such things, explained that "little" Avvo was really in competition with Google and did not have the economy of scale to crack that specific nut, whereas Internet Brands had a better shot at it. Why? Because the investment firm KKR (aka Kohlberg, Kravis, Roberts & Co), a billion-dollar company listed on the New York Stock

---

11 "More Avvo Criticism & Possibly a Way to Game Avvo's Defective Rating System," https://www.charlesakrugel.com/media/more-avvo-criticism-possibly-a-way-to-game-avvo.html, accessed October 26, 2023.

Exchange, owns Internet Brands. And so it goes. Law is lucrative. Venture capital is lucrative.

While looking at Avvo's listing of Albuquerque attorneys, I came across a phenomenon that didn't make much sense. The day I researched that part of the website, Avvo said the City of Albuquerque had 3,432 attorneys, and that Avvo had reviews for 1,779 of them. They ranged from practitioners in business less than a year to others in business for more than half a century.

Avvo's rankings were not in alphabetical order. The first Albuquerque attorney had more than 300 positive reviews and a score of the proverbial "perfect ten." The next lawyer listed had a score of "9.9," but only sixty-five reviews. Both had been licensed for twenty-seven years. The third person had fifty-five reviews, and a score of ten, but had been licensed for only eleven years. As another example, listee number eight had only five reviews (after twenty years in practice) and a score of 9.9, the same as number two on the list. Later, on the same webpage, someone with a 9.3 rating was listed before someone else with a 10 rating.

Takeaway: There's no logical ranking criterion that places attorneys in order on these pages, other than that they have somewhere between four and five stars. It starts to look as if some attorneys might pay more to be listed higher up than others with the same score.

Many of the reviews posted are written by that prolific author "Anonymous." I'm not sure how they vet those people. I've heard some people call Avvo a Yelp for lawyers, but I don't see many complaints for the top-listed firms. (I have seen bitter clients post statements on other sites that Avvo suppresses complaints about favored firms on its own website, and therefore creates biased reviews.)

Avvo has a Better Business Bureau rating of "F" (failing, by the BBB's definition). The few pages of complaints (three of them only) on the BBB's website were posted to little purpose. They come from both lawyers and clients. All date from 2021, and some of the 2021 complaints have not been resolved. It looks as if no one has bothered to post an Avvo complaint on the BBB site since 2021. After stating Avvo's ranking, the BBB website continues, "THIS BUSINESS IS NOT ACCREDITED." The all-capital-letter sentence is theirs, and is printed prominently, in red, on that page.

Because the BBB did not seem to be effective in resolving complaints against Avvo, multiple other protest sites exist. They list all manner of complaints—from inept attorneys who have been disciplined by a judge for their careless work, to lawyers complaining about Avvo's substantial improper charges.

On the positive side, Avvo listings make it easy to get appointments and to find addresses, office hours, and other contact information for attorneys with paid listings. Avvo promises that no attorney material in its directory was created by AI. This is important, because as of this writing, AI still tends to hallucinate and can produce extremely misleading "information." Avvo seems to be the only service in the group reviewed in this book making this "AI-free" claim.

AI doesn't appear to be deeply involved with any of the businesses I've profiled in this book. Perhaps those with extensive blogs and thousands of essays posted do use it. Or maybe they use human ghostwriters. LegalShield doesn't have to prove it isn't using AI. The site itself links to its con-tracted law firms' own websites so humans can help humans. LegalShield's associates' websites are standardized, so no affiliate needs an AI to write essays to post on a website.

Given Avvo's policy of never deleting any names, its lawyer database is likely greatly inflated by outdated listings. On the plus side of the ledger, the amount of free posted research material offered, and the extensive *pro bono* and educational parts of the website are potentially helpful. However, they are not going to give anyone actionable instructions on how to handle a specific case.

Website: https://www.avvo.com

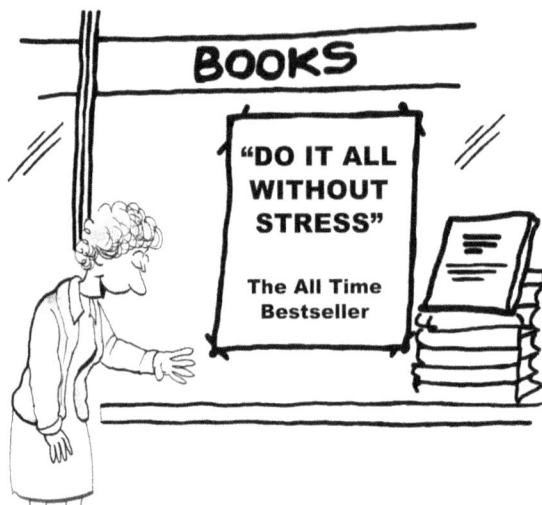

Nolo—The Publishing Company Turned Lawyer Referral Service, with a Side of Software

Nolo.com, its website proclaims, "offers hundreds of consumer-friendly legal products, written in plain English." The company's name comes from a common bit of Latin legal jargon (*nolo contendere*, meaning "I don't argue," also often translated as "no contest"). This company was born of the same impulse as LegalShield—to help those who were not multimillionaires cope with the legal system.

Nolo's founders, Charles Sherman and Ralph Warner, legal aid lawyers in Richmond, California (near Berkeley), met with rejections from commercial publishers. (Back then, it was almost heretical for any attorney to suggest that non-lawyers might be able to read about the law and understand what they read. The publishers also feared pushback from lawyers and bar associations.)

Sherman and Warner formed their own publishing company, originally called Nolo Press. They sold their first books off rented shelves in the produce department of the Berkeley co-op.

The commercial publishers were right—it was inevitable that the Bar Association would complain. At a news conference, the head of the Sacramento Bar condemned Nolo's first title, a book on how to handle your own California divorce, thereby giving the shoestring enterprise priceless publicity. Sales skyrocketed.

Almost no one had filed for a *pro se* divorce in California before 1971. After 800,000 copies of that title were made available for sale and denounced by the Bar, more than 60 percent of the people filing for divorce there did it without the benefit of an attorney.

As Nolo's books became increasingly popular, the U.S. District Court in Texas declared that, under a 1939 Texas law, its legal software constituted practicing law without a license. In a friendly gesture, it suggested that, instead of the court outlawing the software, the legislature might consider changing the law to accommodate Nolo's presence in the marketplace.

Providing information, the Legislature declared, was not illegal, and it was also not the practice of law (providing a statement advised readers that the information was no substitute for an attorney). As you'll discover in a bit more depth in Chapter VIII, it isn't the equivalent of getting legal advice from a licensed attorney.

More and more, Nolo sold its publications over the internet. It rapidly partnered with a dozen or so internet firms in different niches.

The company eventually issued hundreds of books and even a few computer programs. Their subjects range from LLC formation to wills and trusts, with excursions into divorce, tenants' rights, and torts. The company does not always update Amazon listings. A notation next to one of the will-and-trust items says it will take more than twenty-four hours to download using a dial-up modem. Most computer users dispensed with dial-up modems years ago.

Some of the titles run 400-600 pages. Nolo's *Willmaker* software (about which I'll speak more in Chapter VIII) went through eight editions between 1985 and 2000. Its 2023 edition does not specify which edition it is, in relation to the usual "first edition," "second edition," etc., a designation that books carry. These are venerable titles, with a few having gone through as many as nine or more editions, attesting to the company's staying power.

Pay attention to the publication dates. On one of Nolo's Amazon listing pages, reviewers from 2013 and later complain that the item they're reviewing, published in 2004, is out of date. What did they expect? Some outdated Nolo computer programs show up in Amazon listings as well, along with similar criticisms. Perhaps this is what happens when members of a generation accustomed to programs updating themselves automatically come face-to-face with technology from earlier eras. During the Internet Stone Age, you had to buy a new version/update of a program separately. Today, you subscribe, continue to pay an annual fee, and stop worrying.

Legal forms, as well as the laws and rules that underlie them, may change over time. I've offered this caution before, but it's extremely important, so I'll say it again here: You need the most up-to-date information. If you're buying legal forms from 2020, and you're living in 2026, beware. Those forms might well have become outdated within mere months of publication. In most cases, only your attorney (if you have one) will know, for sure, whether they're current and valid.

Nolo started listing attorneys on its website in 2005. Martindale, the legal directory company, entered a joint venture arrangement with Nolo in March 2014. (Martindale-Hubbell, since 1865 a standard directory of legal practitioners, now belongs to legal information provider LexisNexis. The British multi-national behemoth RELX Group—formerly known as Reed-Elsevier—in turn owns Lexis-Nexis.)

If you check back on the corporate lineage tree, you'll see that Lexis-Nexis now owns Martindale-Hubbell, Avvo, Nolo, and several other legal internet brands. Simple Martindale listings are free but will not be included unless the firm submits its own information.

The directory claims over 1 million listings from lawyers and law firms. Some internet sources claim they are worldwide because Martindale-Hubbell's directory is worldwide, but a look at Nolo's site shows only U.S. states listed under geographic areas.

More elaborate listings cost money. Recently, I saw a legal marketing firm explaining to attorneys why they needed to list in Martindale, despite the expense.[12] I've also seen posts on legal marketing sites insisting that the major decision-makers consider "boosted" directory listings a turn-off, instead trying to teach attorneys that awards and other public recognition for their work will attract more and better clients.

If corporate decision-makers resist those enhanced directory listings, why do members of the public fall for them? Does the biggest ad win cases? Or does the victory go to the finest

---

12 "Data Reveals Why You Need to be Listed in Martindale-Hubbell®" https://www.themarketinggurus.com/data-reveals-why-you-need-to-be-listed-in-martindale-hubbell/, posted December 29, 2015, accessed October 26, 2023.

> "If you check back on the corporate lineage tree, you'll see that Lexis-Nexis now owns Martindale-Hubbell, Avvo, Nolo, and several other legal internet brands."

legal mind? I guess this goes back to the mindset promoted by the Yellow Pages people used to get from the old landline phone companies. Often the company with the biggest ad attracted the most new business, regardless of its prowess in its chosen specialty.

As a result of the Martindale-Nolo joint venture, fifty-five categories of attorneys and legal firms have been linked through the Nolo website. This is an attorney matching service, a marketing device that sends the firms your query. But it means you must write about your problem "blind," not knowing much, if anything at all, about who is going to read it. Might it go to a firm that has a conflict of interest with you? Perhaps. They might not technically be allowed to use your information, but that doesn't mean they'll forget what you might have said about the opposing side in your case.

In addition to paying to place the firm's enhanced profile in an online directory, an attorney might also pay to have articles ghostwritten. (As I've mentioned, this also happens with other law marketing services. Some of the downloads you see on law firms' websites might have been written by a ghostwriter). They will also schedule appointments for attorneys. This means that the "back office" you assume is backing up an attorney might not exist.

The Martindale-Nolo partnership promises no special discounts off hourly legal fees or other perks. So, you are not getting any special treatment as a consumer.

Should you choose one of the Martindale-Nolo attorneys, you might find one who has paid per lead, for your inquiry, already has paid for a profile in the directory, pays a ghostwriter to create "lead magnets" (the downloads offered on the firm's website), and who also pays Martindale-Nolo to do all the scheduling. Takeaway: Martindale is making money from offering these services. Attorneys complain (on Reddit and to the Better Business Bureau) that they are not. One attorney claimed to have paid more than $13,000 for "leads" that never materialized.

On its website, Nolo offers articles on legal topics ranging from "accidents" to "workers' compensation." These describe basic legal requirements and theories but do not provide details that will deal with your specific case or any special requirements in your state. Again, you can read a lot about the law, but that doesn't mean it's up to date for your state. Nor does it mean that you'll know how to use that data effectively should you attempt a DIY approach.

Scrolling down through an article on accidents, I discovered that most of the article had been excerpted from a Nolo book on the same subject that has already gone through eleven editions, the most recent of which was 2021. Not too outdated, but also not brand-new material.

If you buy all Nolo's books, it will cost you multiple thousands of dollars. Perhaps you would do better spending that money on having an accomplished attorney take your case. How many 600-page books do you have time to read?

Now, let's say that most of your legal work consists of reading contracts or leases. Or maybe you simply need a lawyer to contact someone, or to give you garden-variety legal advice. In my opinion, it would likely be far more cost-effective, not to mention a far more efficient use of your time, to sign up with a service that will routinely do this for you at no additional fee.

According to its Better Business Bureau web page, Nolo received a 1.57-star rating (out of five). This webpage is contradictory, since it shows only seven reviews (for a company that's been in business for fifty-two years). Below those odd bits of information, the BBB states that thirty-four complaints against Nolo have been closed during the past three years, fourteen of those during the past twelve months. So, the BBB has a lot more information on Nolo, but it is not being offered to consumers.

Trustpilot.com distinguishes between types of ratings, offering on a single list, ratings of Nolo both by the attorneys and by their clients, and also a separate set of reviews of Nolo's publications on the other. The books fare well, rating an aggregate of 4.5 (out of a possible five) for the general quality of the books and forms. On the other hand, 63 percent of both attorneys and clients ranked Nolo's performance in the attorney listing portion of the website low, earning the "matching service" portion of the website a dismal 1.9 rating. One user also had figured out that Nolo outsourced the "chat" section of its site, thereby earning his further condemnation.

Website: https://www.nolo.com/

PERSONAL SERVICE

Quicken—The Digital Will-Writing Service (and Other Programs) Owned by Nolo

It has started to look as if the latter part of this book deals, for the most part, with law services and publishers that resemble those Russian nesting dolls (often called *matryoshka*). That's because we are seeing how individual companies have been absorbed by other companies while maintaining a public presence that makes them seem like independent entities. Most of them *are* like Russian nesting dolls. "Quicken" legal products (as opposed to Quicken accounting and tax products) are really Nolo, which is closely allied with Martindale-Hubbell, which belongs to LexisNexis, which is in turn owned by RELX.

The "Quicken" will-maker, family lawyer, and business lawyer software were not created by the company called "Quicken," as I'll explain below.

Quicken started out providing a personal financial management program. Then the company that owned it quickly branched out into accounting and financial software

(QuickBooks and TurboTax are their flagship programs) for small-to-medium-sized businesses. Back then, in the 1980s, Intuit, Inc, the well-known business software company, owned the Quicken products. Intuit sold Quicken to an investment capital firm in 2016, and that firm sold Quicken to a second one in 2021. Intuit still creates and distributes renowned financial software.

> "If you buy the basic version, and then realize that you need a document that's not included, you'll have to buy that separately. If you want to change your will five years after you complete it, you might need to buy the whole kit again because, without a lawyer's advice, you might not know what's changed in your state."

As I've already mentioned, the will-maker, family lawyer, and business lawyer products were created by Nolo, under a license from Quicken, which is not quite the same thing as being created by Quicken itself. Nolo pays Quicken for the commercial value of calling its products "Quicken," because "Quicken" is a very well-known software company, whereas Nolo is not a well-known software company, although at this point it has sold quite a few law self-help software programs.

The WillMaker Kit is software, and it's still for sale on Amazon. The kit contains a lot of digital questionnaires you'll need to fill out, so if you purchase it, make sure that you've entered all your information correctly. GIGO (garbage in, garbage out), as the adage goes.

The cost of the WillMaker Kit depends on the degree of complexity you select. The list price for "basic" is $99, as of this writing, while the "plus" plan costs $139, and "all access" (which includes thirty-five additional related documents) costs $209. That's for one year and includes a single additional year of software updates. It's a "family pack," meaning that you can also make a will for your spouse, and maybe your Aunt Harriet, as well, if the license allows you to.

If you buy the basic version, and then realize that you need a document that's not included, you'll have to buy that separately. If you want to change your will five years after you complete it, you might need to buy the whole kit again because, without a lawyer's advice, you might not know what's changed in your state.

Are there any automatic problems that come with the kit? Yes. For one, as of this writing the program doesn't work in Louisiana or in any U.S. territories. For another, it's a software download, compatible only with relatively recent versions of Mac and Windows, and available only in English.

If you get confused and want to have an attorney help you, you can't get any legal help through the service department for the program you've just bought. Only customer support (as in, "I'm having trouble downloading this product," or "the software freezes up every time I press this key") is available by phone or email from the company on weekdays, and then only during regular California business hours.

Lawyers list their practices on the Nolo website. You'd always have the option of contacting a lawyer associated with the Nolo (really Martindale-Hubbell) network of attorneys. Does this constitute what marketers refer to as an "upsell" (selling a lower-priced product, mainly to demonstrate to buyers that what they really need is a more expensive, done-for-you, version of the same item)? Perhaps. You wanted to do it yourself, but ultimately discovered that you needed some help after all.

The literature says that Quicken Family Lawyer was developed by a firm named "Parsons Technology," which turns out to have been acquired by Intuit in 1994. What this means, in terms of the Quicken name being licensed to Nolo and Intuit not being responsible for this program, is that you'll likely need a lawyer to explain the nuances of all these machinations to you.

The Texas Committee on the Practice of Law, as we've already seen, took Nolo to court back in 1999, claiming that selling this program constituted the unauthorized practice of law. The product received a 2.7 rating from a total of seven users on Amazon—not promising.

In 2018, a California Appeals Court decision voided a Quicken Family Lawyer-generated prenuptial agreement because the person who had created it was a member of the public, not an attorney. He retained an attorney to explain it to his future wife (and the judge agreed that she had gotten all the information she needed before signing), but apparently figured he was the one using the program, and so didn't need one.

According to the judge, he lacked certain legal information that he should have had prior to signing that document. That knowledge would have been provided to him, as a routine matter, had he consulted a licensed attorney. His ex-wife's signature on that prenup was valid; his was not.

As of late 2023, a notation on the program's Amazon listing page states that this product has been discontinued. Nolo now sells Quicken's own home and business financial management programs on the Nolo website.

Quicken Business Lawyer software can still be found on eBay and is offered on some sites as a free download. If anyone can tell me how to buy it off its listing page on Amazon, I'd be much obliged, because there seems to be no way of accomplishing this feat. The compatible operating systems listed on that page are long obsolete.

Please research your purchase carefully before buying any Nolo-Quicken products that do not have the year of issue in the title. Nolo recently initiated a policy of putting the year for which the program is valid in the title of that program. A program that doesn't have this information is likely an older, perhaps even outdated, program. Since you have no way of knowing what might have changed, it's far safer for you to use either a current program (one that has a year in its title) or an attorney who knows what the latest changes are.

The Quicken WillMaker program is, as I've said, owned by Nolo. In the previous chapter, I gave Nolo's BBB rating, and website information, so there's no reason to repeat that here.

"We're buying the company, the brand, the building ... but mostly we're buying the golden eggs."

Conclusion

You might notice a difference in the service you get depending on whether a firm is public or private, whether it is owed by another company that wants power in a specific profession (in this case law), and so on. To me, the underlying philosophy of the firm itself will also be a major factor. Is that firm's mission customer service, or does it primarily exist to promote attorneys' practices?

Just to recap here, FindLaw is owned by Thompson-Reuters. It makes its main income from the advertising and marketing fees attorneys pay. Avvo also primarily matches attorneys and clients. It earns its primary income from helping attorneys to market their practices to potential clients.

Nolo says the lawyer matching section of its website is a marketing tool for the legal profession.

According to Majux, however, since 2014 there has been no difference between Martindale, LexisNexis, and a third firm not profiled in this book (Lawyers.com). All of them were acquired by Internet Brands that also then owned Nolo. If they are correct, then four of the firms profiled in this book are divisions of the same company. So, Martindale, LexisNexis, and Nolo (Quicken) turn out to be different brand names, rather like the way that Tide, Old Spice, and Vicks are now all brands that belong to Proctor & Gamble. Proctor & Gamble invented Tide, but it bought the Old Spice and Vicks brands.

LegalZoom is a NASDAQ-listed corporation. Its forms might or might not be current.

Rocket Lawyer, still a private corporation, focuses on business law. Some people say Rocket Lawyer's DIY library is easier to use than LegalZoom's, and that Rocket Lawyer is cheaper. LegalZoom will require you to fill out forms stating the details of your purpose every time you want to download something. As of this writing, Rocket Lawyer allows you to use the same form multiple times, no questions asked.

Most firms profiled earlier that started by providing services or forms only to business founders and owners have begun to branch out into what is, for them, new territory—consumer legal help. For them, this is an experiment, or at least this new work consists of services they haven't fully explored before.

Only two of the firms profiled earlier have retained their original mission as their primary focus—LegalShield and Rocket Lawyer. Of the two, LegalShield was always firmly consumer-oriented, and Rocket Lawyer always had a corporate mindset. Although LegalShield now services home-based businesses and has branched out into selling its services as perks for corporate employees, Rocket Lawyer has not broadened its operations.

LegalShield's goal differs fundamentally from that of the corporations that were formed as, or became through corporate mergers and acquisitions, marketing devices for the thousands of independent attorneys and law firms that they list. It also differs from the ones (like Nolo) that might have started with a DIY mentality but later morphed into providing marketing opportunities for attorneys.

As I said in Chapter I, LegalShield joined a portfolio of companies when it was bought out by MidOcean. Several of the other firms also owned by Mid-Ocean provide service-oriented activities too—dental practices, healthcare staffing, and the like. LegalShield's basic philosophy has remained one of providing attorneys' services on demand and at reasonable cost compared to what other services charge. That has remained consistent.

This book has allowed you to get to know the top five DIY and prepaid legal services. Now, you can also compare those with what Avvo and Nolo provide. I hope that the information you've found here assists you in deciding whether what these companies provide will meet your needs. If you've found *Legal Protection* helpful, please leave a review of this volume here.

Acknowledgements

Thanks are due to many people who helped me prepare this book for publication. First, I'm grateful to author and coach extraordinaire Jack Canfield for his enthusiastic support of this book idea, and to marketing guru Steve Harrison, who encouraged me to think that the information included here might help a great many people.

On the legal side, I'd especially like to thank David A. Garcia, Esq. and James E. Dory, Esq. for consulting with me about LegalZoom. Later in the process, James L. Foust and Charles L. McElwee walked me through the processes and policies of LegalShield. I greatly appreciate James L. Foust's offer to help me find real humans to walk those with questions through the LegalShield website. Thanks also to Scott E. Scioli for general consultation about legal services.

All five firms on the "Five Best" list (and the "Bonus Firms" Avvo and Nolo, as well) made mountains of information available on their websites. They've separately published explanations of how attorneys receive listings and other promotional considerations from them. I also benefitted greatly from independent rating firms and organizations (like the Better Business Bureau and TrustPilot) that also post reviews, as well as additional websites totally unrelated to the businesses themselves where people discuss their experiences dealing with these companies.

I'm grateful to Judy Peterson and Simon Hale, who served as first readers.

A special vote of appreciation to Cristina Smith (publishing and marketing coach), Valerie Costa (editor), and Christy Day (book design) and Maggie McLaughlin (ebook and technical support) for their help in preparing the draft for publication. Finally, thanks to Steve Scholl for his expert proofreading.

About the Author

Born in New York City, **Léonie Rosenstiel** has traveled to four continents (if you count Central America). She admits to having spent "a lot of time" in school, earning degrees in fields as diverse as musicology, public health, ministry, and East Asian medicine. Her life journey has also brought her into frequent contact with attorneys, in large part because she spent long periods as a caregiver for her husband and her mother—nine years each.

Léonie regularly teaches and speaks to groups, and she coaches and consults with individuals and families. She has interviewed attorneys, judges, "professional" guardians, and caregivers to discover both the problems and the possible solutions to the difficulties people have when confronting family issues.

She is the author of *Protecting Mama: Surviving the Legal Guardianship Swamp*, that has won four different literary awards. She also created the *Dayspring Empowerment*

Summit and the *Dayspring Empowerment Course*. She often participates as a panelist, and is also a popular podcast guest. To contact her, email leonie@dayspringresources.com. Visit her website at https://DayspringResources.com.

Léonie now lives in Albuquerque, New Mexico, where she loves to nurse a cup of Earl Grey tea while watching the sunrise over the Sandia Mountains.

Check out the author's other activities and publications:

- *Protecting Mama: Surviving the Legal Guardianship Swamp* (Calumet Editions)

- *Nadia Boulanger: A Life in Music* (W. W. Norton)

- Website: https://DayspringResources.com

- Contact email: leonie@dayspingresources.com

- Dayspring Resources, Inc. offers techniques and coaching to families (see website for more details) and helps to teach the families of elders to become Resilient Transition Planners.

Léonie Rosenstiel is available for interviews and frequently speaks to online groups. Contact her at the email above for more information. Please let her know whether there are other subjects you'd like her to research.

www.ingramcontent.com/pod-product-compliance
Lightning Source LLC
Chambersburg PA
CBHW060253030426
42335CB00014B/1679